SAN FRANCISCO

Designed and Produced by

Ted Smart & David Gibbon

MAYFLOWER BOOKS · NEW YORK CITY

Introduction: The Paradoxical Paradise

SAN FRANCISCO is a city of paradoxes: built on the best anchorages on the west coast of North America it is plagued by fogs that made navigation hazardous until the discovery of radar; safely isolated on its peninsula, it is constantly threatened by the weakness of the earth's crust beneath it; settled as a quiet agricultural community, it became a city as the result of the Gold Rush of 1849 and the discovery of silver in Nevada; evolved as a center of humanitarian and liberal culture which gave birth to the Flower Children and their philosophy of love, it has become a center of drug peddling and addiction; blessed by a setting and climate that should make its inhabitants the happiest people on earth, it has the highest suicide, divorce and alcoholism rates in the United States.

These hazards do not appear to diminish the zest with which San Franciscans live their lives. In fact, one might guess that they thrive on them, just as their ancestors did on the perils and adventures involved in reaching the Golden West.

The layout of the city, planned by Swiss designer Jean Jacques Vioget in 1839, is symbolic of the lifestyle of San Francisco. Despite the steep hills which make up the peninsula, at whose northern extremity is the famous Golden Gate Bridge, the streets form an inflexible grid which sends some of them up hill and down dale in a series of ascents and descents reminiscent of a roller coaster. A popular location for car chases in police thriller movies, the streets also give riders of San Francisco cable cars some moments of breathtaking excitement as well as superb views of the Bay.

The cable cars are themselves symbols of a kind and, despite modern traffic conditions and more suitable means of public transport, no San Franciscan would part with them. Though no longer as numerous as in the past, the cable cars still run east and west along California Street and north to south along Powell and Hyde Streets, clanging their bells at every intersection and claiming a right-of-way that no one would dare dispute.

Market Street is a key street in the design of the city; running from southwest to northeast across the eastern side of the city, it forms an angle with Van Ness Avenue, which runs due north and south. Between the two streets is contained the liveliest and richest part of the city's life.

In a distinctive blend of old and new, the gabled houses of Steiner Street on pages 4 and 5 stand outlined against the high rise blocks of modern San Francisco.

Nestling in the Japanese Tea Garden of the Golden Gate Park, clear pools left, reflect with exotic artistry the dwarf trees that line their banks.

In the southern angle of the triangle lies the Civic Center, a spacious area laid out with lawns and parks among which rise dignified buildings where federal, state and city authorities carry out their responsibilities. During the day this is a quarter where people go about their business in the quiet and routine manner suited to civic surroundings, but even here the cheerful spirit of San Francisco comes to the fore from time to time. One of these times is in spring when the trees are in blossom and an open-air art show provides a colorful display of human ingenuity and imagination.

Art is very much a part of the Civic Center. Among its eight major buildings, which include the Renaissance style City Hall, is the War Memorial Opera House which is the home of the San Francisco Opera, the San Francisco Symphony Orchestra and the Ballet. Many fine artistic performances have taken place in the Opera House, but the most momentous event of all was the signing of the United Nations Charter there in 1945.

On gala nights, the Opera House still recalls some of the dazzle of the Belle Époque when famous singers like Tetrazzini entertained San Francisco society. In those rough pioneering days, when San Francisco possessed one of the toughest, bawdiest quarters of any city in America, it also stood out as a center of culture. The cultural side had been built up by the many Europeans who had come to San Francisco in search of a new life, and the foundation they laid is still basic in the city's life.

The contrast between the two aspects of the city's life is in keeping with the paradoxical nature of San Francisco itself, much of whose charm today lies in the unexpected contrasts of its streets. Compare, for example, the character of the buildings around Union Square, the traditional center of the city, with those of Chinatown, only a few blocks away up Grant Avenue. At Union Square, and the surrounding Powell, Stockton, Geary and O'Farrell Streets, are the smartest shops and restaurants, jewelers, flower shops and flower stands along the sidewalks, reflecting the changing seasons in a riot of color. There is a certain formality about the shoppers here; the ladies often wear hats and the men stopping to buy a bouquet for one of them at the flower stalls are conventionally attired. Even Maiden Lane on the east side of the Square has forgotten its wicked past as the street of brothels and looks demure with its line of trees and little boutiques.

Chinatown is quite different. Here the buildings have an exotic sweep to them and the shop windows are festooned with Oriental goods, or if they are food shops, with shiny glazed ducks or strings of Chinese candies. Most of the faces peering into the windows with amazement and delight will be those of tourists, but even the San Franciscan can become a tourist from time to time as he explores his own city.

Another contrast nearby is Montgomery Street, a thoroughfare made to seem narrow by the office buildings that rise like the side of a concrete canyon into the sky. This is the Wall Street of the West and in and around it are the banks, insurance companies and brokerage firms where business life hums all day long and sometimes into the night. Among the tall buildings are the Bank of America which rises to 779 feet in 52 stories, and the Wells Fargo Building slightly lower at 43 stories. The latter company played an important part in the business life of the early West when it transported the gold and silver which had brought fortune to the businessmen who supplied the prospectors' needs.

There is plenty of historical interest in this part of San Francisco, for this is where the first settlement began to grow. The very first house was built at Clay Street, when the settlement was still known as Yerba Buena, a name the Spaniards gave it because of the abundance of a sweet-smelling herb which grew there. Farther along Clay Street is Portsmouth Square where Captain John Montgomery planted the U.S. flag and claimed the land for the United States in 1846. Perhaps it was this stirring event that appealed to the imagination of Robert Louis Stevenson, who liked to sit and dream in the grassy square when he lived in San Francisco.

A little farther north is a quarter which lives up to the paradox that is San Francisco; once it was the Barbary Coast, a name that has sounded round the world as a symbol of violence and vice. On the Barbary Coast, the roughest elements among the gold seekers, the sailors and the tough men who pioneered the West would gather to have a wild time. Prostitution was rife, with young Chinese girls pressed into the profession, and murders were so common that few of the perpetrators were brought to justice. Today the Barbary Coast is an area of smartly restored build-ings and shops. A few blocks to the north is another paradox—the quarter known as North Beach, though there is no sign of sea or sand. This is inhabited by San Francisco's peace-loving Italians, whose main concern appears to be to build a little Italy in the surrounding streets. Everywhere there are food shops, their counters laden with spaghetti, pizzas, cheeses, olives and all the other delicious ingredients of Italian cooking. Behind the counters stand the Italian ladies, looking as if they have just been transported from Naples and ready for an argument or a discussion about the quality of the products they sell.

This is one aspect of North Beach; another has echoes of the wicked old days. At Broadway and Columbus the night scene is one of flashing neon, sidewalk cafés, striptease parlors and jazz clubs. The famed San Francisco liberal spirit runs riot here,

though today one does not walk in danger of one's life, or of being shanghaied and waking up a member of the crew on a ship bound for China.

North Beach is to San Francisco what Soho is to London or Montmartre to Paris: a place of entertainment with tourists in mind. The regular residents have them in mind, too, so here one finds little shops where crafts are on sale and the craftsmen who make them live quiet working lives in the neighborhood.

To the southwest of the noisy, frenetic area around Columbus is the quiet, residential quarter of Nob Hill where two cable car routes cross. Near its summit, there are splendid views across to Russian Hill and beyond to Telegraph Hill with its tower which was built, some say, in the shape of a fire hose to commemorate the enthusiasm of Lillie Hitchcock Coit, its donor, for the city's firemen.

The triangle formed by Market Street and Van Ness Avenue opens out towards the Bay in the north: here there is a great sweep of quays stretching from the Oakland Bay Bridge on the east side to famous Fisherman's Wharf on the north. Beyond that along the coast lies the Golden Gate Bridge.

For the visitor, the north waterfront is the most fascinating part of San Francisco, as it is intended to be. Once busy with shipping, it decayed when the steamers' role as the main means of transport was taken over by rail and then by air transport; now it has been transformed into a playground in which memories of the past are cleverly linked with the practicalities of the present. At its western end lie two startling examples of the conversion of obsolete buildings. One is the chocolate factory at Ghirardelli Square. In the red brick buildings where chocolate was once produced, there are now art galleries, theaters, restaurants, and shops that sell jewelry and clothes imported from all over the world. The outdoor cafés are crowded in summer and part of the show is provided by the chefs who spin out paperthin pancakes or create ice cream sundaes as fantastic as the setting of Fisherman's Wharf.

The other converted building is The Cannery, a far cry now from the Del Monte factory where workers once packed the fruit from California orchards. Today's Cannery is a three-level shopping complex where goods can be bought ranging from primitive art to pet foods. From the top of the building there are fine views over city and harbor, including a sight of the notorious Alcatraz Island prison which once housed such infamous criminals as Al Capone and Machine Gun Kelly. Alcatraz itself is another of the San Francisco paradoxes, for it never found enough of the tough tenants it was designed to house and so became an ordinary prison full of small-time crooks. The cost of maintaining them in the island fortress became prohibitive and the prison was phased out of use in the 1960's.

The fame of Fisherman's Wharf rests on many of the same reasons as that of Santa Lucia in Naples. Here is a dock on which the restaurants ply a busy trade and the smell of frying and grilling fish fills the air. The view, when there is no fog, is sublime and stretches from the red structure of the Golden Gate Bridge to the land across the Bay. In the harbor, little boats and yachts bob at their anchors and along the sidewalks there are stalls that sell everything imaginable. As in Naples, the air is filled with the songs and music of itinerant musicians and romance is in the air.

A genuine touch of the old seafaring life remains at the eastern end of the Wharf where the *Balclutha,* a three-masted sailing ship that used to sail from Britain to San Francisco via Cape Horn, is moored and is now a museum. Nearby is another historic vessel, but this time a replica: the *Golden Hinde* of Sir Francis Drake which was built in Devon only a few years ago and sailed across to America in an evocation of the original voyage.

There are still more ships to be found at the Hyde Street Pier, for those who feel nostalgic for the old days when ships were more than mere symbols of adventure. This is San Francisco's Maritime State Historic Park and along the length of the pier are schooners, ferry boats and a steam tug. To clinch the maritime character of this part of the city, there is the Aquatic Park Maritime Museum which is packed with objects taken off old ships, including figureheads, anchors and binnacles.

From Aquatic Park starts one of the finest walks in San Francisco: along the Golden Gate Promenade west to Fort Point, which was built to defend the city and is now a museum. On the heights above the walk are some of the most expensive houses in San Francisco and on the sea before them some of their owners' luxurious yachts. Along this stretch of the waterfront are also the Presidio, where the Spaniards set up their garrison in 1776, and the weather-worn splendor of the Palace of Fine Arts, built as a temporary edifice for the 1915 Exhibition, which no one has had the heart to take down.

Although closely packed with its houses marching up and down the hills in close formation, San Francisco never seems constricted like other large cities. From its slopes there are always sweeping views across the bay or sea and overhead the sky stretches endlessly towards the mountains and over the Pacific. Nevertheless, the creators of the city have taken care to provide those open spaces essential in any urban area. The most important of these is Golden Gate Park, converted by John McLaren from a wild sweep of sand-dunes into a park that is the joy of all San Franciscans. During weekdays visitors can park their cars anywhere along the drives that traverse the park but on weekends, except for John Kennedy Drive, the pedestrian is king.

The western end of the park is fringed by the Pacific Ocean whose great waves crash along the beach beyond the Great Highway. At its eastern end Haight Street, of Haight Ashbury and Flower Children fame, connects with Market Street which runs through San Francisco to the Bay waterfront at Embarcadero. In the park there are bridle paths, bicycle tracks, lakes and museums. Buffalo and elk roam freely in a special area and by the M.H. de Young Museum, with its special wing that houses the Asian Art Collection of Avery Brundage, is a Japanese Tea garden. Every detail of the three-acre site has been carefully designed to simulate a Japanese Garden and includes a temple, a bridge, gateways, a Buddha and even a teahouse where tea is served by Japanese ladies in national costume.

In another part of the park the atmosphere is very English, with a splendid white-painted iron and glass greenhouse like the one at Kew Gardens by the Thames, sitting elegantly amid the foliage.

In the center of the city lies Twin Peaks, a tall hill with a 65-acre park which is a favorite viewpoint with visitors and residents. From here there is a bird's-eye view of the whole city, including the Bay and the Golden Gate and Oakland bridges, stretching away to the Marin shore in the north and to the island of Yerba Buena and then on to Oakland in the northeast. To the west lies the Pacific and to the south the spectacular coastline of Monterey and Big Sur.

From a high viewpoint such as this it is easy to see why the bridges feature so largely in San Francisco's mind; they are the lifelines between the city and the rest of the land around the Bay. Before they were built, all transport across the Bay was by ferryboat. The bridges gradually put the ferries out of business, though one has come back into operation in recent years. The bridge connecting San Francisco to Oakland was completed in 1936 and today carries the commuter traffic from Oakland. The overall length of the bridge is eight and a quarter miles and it has a two-deck structure carrying one-way traffic on each level. At Yerba Buena Island, where it dives through a tunnel, there is a magnificent view of San Francisco for motorists who are traveling west; a view that is even more unforgettable at night.

Though Oakland Bay Bridge is a complex structure as well as the world's longest steel bridge, it is the Golden Gate Bridge, opened in 1937, that is the symbol of San Francisco. The graceful silhouette of the bridge has appeared in millions of vacation photos and movies, and over thirty million vehicles cross it every year. To most people it is the most potent of all the images of San Francisco, representing a gateway to adventure and new ideas which, when the sea mist rolls in and wraps itself around the span, appears as two stairways leading skywards into an infinite space.

The dizzy vantage point of Twin Peaks overleaf, provides a breathtaking view of Market Street and downtown San Francisco.

Beneath the Golden Gate Bridge, the rugged rocks and sparkling waters of the San Francisco Bay provide an ideal resort for seals and surfers alike. To the people who live on its shores, the bay is an expanse of water to be cherished, protected and above all, enjoyed.

At the heart of the city overleaf, rise the skyscrapers of the financial district, from which an impressive portion of world finance is controlled.

Spanning the historic Golden Gate of San Francisco, the Golden Gate Bridge on these pages and overleaf, is the tallest and largest single span suspension bridge in the world. In defiance of the inconsistencies of the elements a 90ft wide traffic deck and two pedestrian walks are miraculously suspended above the ever-shifting moods of the waters below.

Gateway to Glamor

THE star quality of the city of San Francisco is not enhanced, as with others which rival it for the title of the most beautiful city in the world, because it outshines its environment. Rather, it is the crown in a setting of dazzling beauty. All around it are places that in their own way are as exciting and breathtaking as the city itself.

Scenically, the locations within reach of San Francisco are on the grand scale: forests of giant redwood trees, sheer mountains and staggeringly dramatic coastline built on a titanic scale. In this setting it is not surprising to find the human contribution also larger than life, for that is a manner that human beings adopt to avoid being dwarfed by the environment.

Randolph Hearst, the famous emperor of a vast world of publishing, built himself a castle palace at San Simeon down the coast, and filled it with artistic treasures as if to defy the ever-present reminder of man's insignificance in the face of nature. On the other hand, around Big Sur, a town amid awe-inspiring scenery, the artists and philosophers take the view that if you can't beat it you'd better join it and cultivate fatalistic Oriental philosophies.

But size is not everything in the fabulous countryside around San Francisco Bay. Small, too, is beautiful and packs a punch in such places as Sausalito, a small harbor that reminds one of those picturesque villages along the Mediterranean where houses are piled up the tree-covered hillsides and the masts of yachts create an artificial forest by the water's edge.

Sausalito is frankly for tourists but its charm is no less for that. Little shops in colorfully painted houses make temptation irresistible and the views from the terraces of the many restaurants are superb.

For those who find artificial picturesqueness too cloying and long for nature in the raw, it is only an hour's drive into another world where the coastal redwoods (Sequoia sempervirens) grow in impressive solitude. These giants of the tree world (the tallest recorded is 365 feet and the oldest over 2000 years of age) flourish on the coast and on the high Sierra, though the latter are of the *giganteum* variety.

There are many stands of redwoods along the coasts north and south of San Francisco and in the national parks such as the Redwood National Park, on the coast at the northern limit of California, and the Sequoia National Park inland to the southeast near another Californian marvel, the Yosemite National Park. The nearest to San Francisco are in Muir Woods along the banks of Redwood Creek at the southern part of Mount Tamalpais, an area which is extremely popular with San Franciscans for walking.

Circling the Bay in a clockwise direction from Mount Tamalpais, one comes to a region dear to wine-lovers. Here, in Napa and Sonoma, are the vineyards that produce much of California's wine. Here, too, as in other parts of the San Francisco area, are echoes of the Mediterranean. In the midst of the neat rows of vines are houses that could have been plucked straight out of the Bordeaux region of France, and, as in that hospitable place, the vineyards are happy to receive visitors and to invite them to taste the local product. St Helena, the center of the wine trade, offers, with that talent for surprising one which is typical of the area, mud baths and geysers including California's Old Faithful which blows a 50-foot stream of hot vapor into the air every fifty minutes. These lie near Calistoga, the town next to St Helena.

The East Bay is reached from San Francisco by the Oakland Bay Bridge which takes one into Oakland, the largest city in the East Bay. Many of San Francisco's commuters live on this side of the Bay and many of their children go to the University of California at Berkeley. The University spreads up into the low hills and is dominated by a campanile which would be equally at home in Venice.

Another world-famous university lies to the south of the San Francisco peninsula; this is Stanford, at Palo Alto. It, too, has a tower, this time of a Moorish rather than Italian style, that marks the location of the Hoover Institution of War, Revolution and Peace.

Much of the glamor and spectacle that one associates with the Californian coast lies farther south on State Highway Number One which follows the coast past the San Mateo State beaches and the town of Santa Cruz, which contains some fine examples of Victorian architecture, to Monterey.

If gold had not been discovered near San Francisco, Monterey might well have been the most important port on California's west coast. The same Gaspar de Portola who discovered San Francisco, and Father Serra, who built the mission there, also founded Monterey which, until the middle of the nineteenth century, was the most important settlement on that part of the coast.

In modern Monterey there is still plenty of evidence of Spanish and Mexican influence. Eleven of the old buildings are carefully preserved, including the Presidio, the Customs House, and the Casa del Oro, a gold repository. There is also Cannery Row, immortalized by John Steinbeck in his novel of the same name. Today, Steinbeck's house in nearby Salinas is a restaurant and Cannery Row a street of art galleries and antique shops, but one or two vestiges of the old Cannery Row remain, such as the Chinese grocery store where the characters in the book bought their food and drink.

Monterey and Carmel, just south along the point covered by the Del Monte Forest along the shores of which are the rocks and windswept pines familiar to every movie-goer, are both vacation resorts. Their efforts to remain simple, unspoilt places stimulate the desire of tourists to visit them. This is particularly true of Carmel, which with its beautiful beach, its facilities for everything from horseback riding to golf, its artists' colony and smart boutiques has the same studied and sophisticated simplicity as St Tropez on the French Riviera.

Like the rest of the area around San Francisco, these once-quiet villages may be fighting a losing battle to preserve the charm that makes them so attractive to their despoilers, but that is in the nature of life for many such places in glamorous parts of the world.

Built where everyone said a bridge could not be built, the Golden Gate Bridge left, is a triumphant monument to modern engineering.

Level after level of homes overleaf, stairstep up the hills in a city apparently stacked up on itself.

In constructing the 20th century giants above, or the imposing Union Square overleaf, beneath which lies one of the world's largest underground parking lots, the historical has not been altogether lost: Alcatraz Island left, was once the site of the most dreaded penitentiary in the U.S., Fort Point below, built in 1861 to guard the Golden Gate, remains half-concealed under the south tower of the Golden Gate Bridge and Hyde Street Pier right, gives access to historic ships.

Land is precious in a city virtually surrounded by water. From the tip of Twin Peaks or of Coit Tower on Telegraph Hill the density with which San Francisco's buildings, old and new, are packed together, becomes strikingly apparent. Aware of the need to conserve space even the city's early residential areas overleaf, were composed of small houses with gardens and landscaped pathways almost hidden from the stranger's eye.

Without water on three sides, San Francisco right, would possibly be just one more conglomerate of buildings, streets and people, but relative inaccessibility has helped to make this place conspicuously different. Even the most recently constructed buildings like Transamerica's pyramidal 'skysaver' on these pages, reaching from the city's concrete congestion towards an almost cloudless sky, have their own distinctive character.

From Yerba Buena to San Francisco

AFTER the destruction of the Aztec Empire, the Spanish conquistadores began the exploration of the new continent they had discovered. A new fleet of ships was built and began the vain search for a passage which would, they thought, lead them through to the East Indies. But it was not until 1775 that a ship sailed into the most beautiful bay on the west coast of America. The ship was the *San Carlos* and its Captain Don Manual Ayala arrived to chart the bay.

Six years previously, the bay had been seen from land by a force under Gaspar de Portola and now, following the charting of the bay, the Spaniards attempted to establish a settlement with some two hundred people under the command of Captain Juan Bautista de Anza. The place they founded was named Yerba Buena, after a sweet-smelling herb they found there, and for many years it consisted of nothing but a mission building surrounded by adobe houses. Life was easy at Yerba Buena; the warm sun and the moisture from the mists that blew in from the sea made fruit trees and vegetables thrive, and on the vast expanses of land that sloped away from the bay there was plenty of room and pasture for sheep and cattle.

This little Eden received few outside visitors, though occasionally a trapper or a hunter from the mainland would arrive to trade his furs or a whaler would put in with his ship. In 1846, the Spanish conquerors began to suffer the same fate as the Indians whom they had dispossessed. This time, the invaders were Americans from the East who came to establish their own claims to this part of the continent.

When the Yankee ship *Portsmouth,* under Captain John Montgomery, arrived at Yerba Buena, the town's 200 inhabitants made no effort to resist when he planted the Stars and Stripes on the peninsula where the town stood. No doubt for them, as for most ordinary people concerned with making a living, one flag was much like another.

By 1847, there were 450 inhabitants in the little town and its name had been changed to San Francisco. Still, life was quiet and the little settlement might have gone on in this way for years except for one event. In 1849, a man called Marshall, working at Sutters Mill in the Sierra Hills, found gold. At first, no one took much notice but then it was realized that he had struck a rich vein of the precious metal. Within two years, the population of San Francisco had grown to 25,000 and the bay was full of ships that had brought the hopeful emigrants who headed inland to the gold fields.

San Francisco became the center of the gold rush fever, crowded with new arrivals or with those who looked for distractions after weeks in the Sierras. Some were full of hope, some desperate at not finding the gold they had gambled their lives on, and all looked for somewhere to stay, a place to eat and bars that offered wine, women and song. San Francisco was soon full of people prepared to provide these amenities and the place rapidly gained a reputation for violence and garish gaiety that survives today. In such an environment, it is not surprising that murders were daily occurrences and prostitution a flourishing business.

In self-defense, or to guard their private interests, the San Franciscans formed bodies of citizens who took the law into their own hands. These were the famous Vigilantes who soon degenerated into rival gangs, whose concern was to guard the interests of their own supporters and encourage the destruction of rival groups. Soon the violence burned itself out, the gold was exhausted and San Francisco began to settle down to a more orderly life.

Those who had carefully accumulated the money that the miners threw around so recklessly settled down to run the businesses they had started during the Gold Rush. One of the most romantic of the companies which had served the Forty-Niners, as the gold prospectors were called, was the Wells Fargo Company. Operating as an Express and Banking company, Wells Fargo had transported passengers to and from San Francisco during the Gold Rush and had carried back the gold for those who had been lucky enough to strike it rich.

Wells Fargo soon had another valuable cargo to transport; this time it was silver. In the Washoe silver mines, a huge strata of silver was discovered; this was the famous Comstock Lode which made the fortunes of still more San Franciscans. The new rich became the high society of San Francisco and the houses they built on Nob Hill were designed to outdo each other as grandiose monuments. One of them had no less than 437 baths and covered two and a half acres.

Between the ostentatious vulgarity of the new rich on Nob Hill and the gaudy licentiousness of the poor in the part of the town known as the Barbary Coast, a more cultured San Francisco was being born. This was due in some measure to the arrival of European immigrants who brought with them the culture of the Old World and introduced a taste for literature, music and the arts.

The theater flourished and, since money was plentiful, the foremost artists from Europe appeared in San Francisco, among them Sarah Bernhardt, Isadora Duncan, Madame Tetrazzini and Lillie Langtry, though the latter was perhaps more notorious for her affairs than famous for her talent. A University was founded by Leland Stanford – Stanford University – and standards of cuisine, entertainment and other good things of life improved enormously.

In 1906, this self-confident, affluent, easy-going world came to an abrupt and violent end. The earthquake that brought the city down began at 5.13 a.m. on 18 April, and what the earthquake did not wreck, the fire that followed consumed. Out of a population of about 350,000 a quarter of a million were made homeless and 500 died.

The pioneering spirit did not die, however, and the city continued to be known for its liberal attitudes and adventurous spirit. In recent times it has been the breeding ground for youth movements that have spread through the world – the Flower Children was one such; but what the city itself deems its proudest moment was when it was chosen as the site for the birth of the United Nations in 1945.

The whimsical mermaid fountain left, *designed by Ruth Asawa forms the focal point of the famous Ghirardelli Square.*

Yachts and cruising boats overleaf, *lie at their luxurious moorings in the dappled waters of the marina.*

In Ghirardelli Square left, a 70 year-old chocolate factory has been remodelled to house exclusive shops, art galleries, elegant restaurants and even a theater.

Fisherman's Wharf on this page, is the embarking and landing point of San Francisco's many fishermen. Picturesque and in some respects bizarre, it is world-renowned for its fine sea food.

Beyond Fisherman's Wharf overleaf, Coit Tower on Telegraph Hill rises in a shape intended to resemble a firehose nozzle as a tribute to Lillie Hitchcock Coit, who took such an interest in the Volunteer Fire Department.

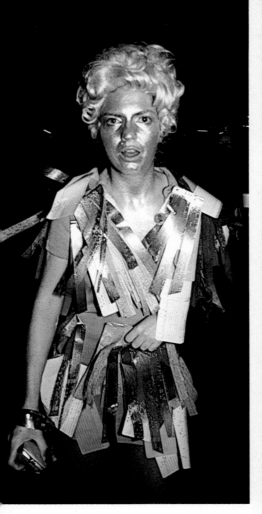

Outdoor murals like those left, by Mujeres Muralistas, three women artists, brighten walls and fences in the Mission District.

Extravagant costumes above and below are an essential feature of a Hookers' Ball in Cow Palace and, also on display in Cow Palace, turbo charged engines and polished vintage cars below right and above right, reflect the skill and care of a bygone era.

San Francisco, Here They Came

IN the quiet, sunny village of pre-Gold Rush days, the inhabitants of San Francisco included some of the original Spaniards who had stayed on after Captain Montgomery raised the U.S. flag and some of the Americans who were looking for new places to settle. A few were sailors who had arrived by ship, liked the beauty of the place and settled down; some of these were Chinese, others Hawaiian and still others came from central Chile, a land not unlike California.

Then James Marshall found gold at Sutters Mill. Within a year or two San Francisco became a sprawling, boisterous, shanty town as immigrants from war-torn Europe, and other parts of the world, came to find the wealth that would put an end to poverty. Not many found it, but among those who did were the clever ones who, rather than prospecting for gold, began satisfying the demands set up by the growing community which soon numbered 25,000 people.

There were houses to be built, mouths to be fed, laundry to be done and roads to be built, and the newcomers set about the various jobs with the talents natural to their nations. The Italians took easily to catering – and they still do. They are the biggest ethnic community in San Francisco, living mostly in the area between Columbus, with its garish night life, and Fisherman's Wharf on the north waterfront.

Many of today's San Franciscans of Italian origin play an important part in the city's administration, but the bulk of them live much the same lives as they would in Italy. Family is the mainstay of their society and Washington Square is the center of their community. Here they have a church of Saint Peter and Paul to remind them of all the other Peter and Paul churches in their native land. In the shops and restaurants, most of them with display signs in Italian, Italian cheeses and salamis and the aroma of garlic fills the air; in the backrooms the mamas and aunts roll out the pastas and do the washing and ironing in much the same way as they might have in Italy.

The next largest ethnic community in the city is the Chinese. They, too, have taken over a part of the city and made it their own; in fact, San Francisco's Chinatown is so renowned that a special chapter is devoted to it.

The Japanese community has left its mark on the city in the nicest possible way by inspiring the charming Japanese Garden in Golden Gate Park and by building the imposing Japanese Center which spreads over three blocks west of Van Ness Avenue on Geary and Post Streets. The centerpiece of the complex of buildings is a five-story pagoda dedicated to friendship and good will between the Japanese people and United States; it was built in 1968 and symbolizes the new understanding between Japan and America that followed World War II.

Japanese expertise in the making of transistors and cameras is displayed in the showrooms around the pagoda, but a more fascinating glimpse of Japanese customs is provided by such entertainments as the Japanese Theater and the festivals, the most colorful of which is the Cherry Blossom Festival in the spring. Though not strictly an entertainment, the Kabuki Hot Springs also provide an authentically Japanese atmosphere and in the steamy atmosphere of the bath tubs and rest rooms, East meets West in the relaxed manner that is typically San Franciscan.

Today's San Franciscan of Japanese origin is a good businessman who takes part in the city's business life as well as running restaurants where the delicate flavors of sukiyaki and tempura cooking are enhanced by the prettiness of the kimono-clad waitresses who serve them.

But what of the original inhabitants – the Mexicans, Spaniards and Americans who settled in the early city? They are still there, administrating the city from the Civic Center, keeping the wheels of finance turning on Montgomery Street, or running the shops and boutiques around Union Square. In fact, apart from the markedly ethnic communities, where not all the members of each reside – only half of San Francisco's Chinese live in Chinatown – the city is a mixture of races all living in relative peace and tolerance with each other.

Relics of the original settlers are evident in the names of streets – Quintara Street, for instance, or Serra Boulevard, named after the priest who founded the first mission in California in 1769.

Sutter Street, today a smart shopping street, commemorates the man on whose land the gold that brought thousands upon thousands of hopeful people from all over the world to San Francisco was first found.

In more recent times, America's blacks, who had formerly represented only a small percentage of the population, have come to San Francisco in increasing numbers. They first moved in during World War II when they came to work in the nearby wartime industries, and they took over many of the streets formerly occupied by the Japanese who had been moved into camps. The black population has continued to grow and lives beside all the other people of every race and color who make up the community of San Francisco.

In this great melting pot of a city, life has the same easygoing cosmopolitan flavor which is found in other integrated cities, such as Paris and London. On the whole, however, people live together peaceably, crowding the transport systems during the commuter rush, hanging to the cable cars with nonchalant ease, inspecting the produce in the market places and the goods in the shops or just gathering in the parks and squares in their leisure time.

Visitors and tourists make up another community, though a transient one, and they add to the life of the city by creating a demand for entertainment and catering which benefits the San Franciscan both in revenue for the city and in the amenities available.

It is not without reason that the San Franciscan feels himself different from other city dwellers and takes an easygoing, philosophical view of life; he knows that he lives in a city set in one of the most beautiful and fruitful parts of the earth. He may occasionally compare it with Naples, Hong Kong, or Rio de Janeiro, but he is unlikely ever to want to change it for any of them.

Colorful figures like the clown-faced street musician left, bring life and character to the San Francisco streets.

Stanford University center left, *founded in 1883 by railroad baron Leland Stanford and his wife in memory of their son, encompasses 8,200 acres. The Memorial Church* above left and below left, *with its exquisite Venetian mosaics and stained glass windows* overleaf, *lies at the heart of the campus in a quadrangle of sandstone buildings.*

The University of California in Berkeley above and far right *and its famous Campanile are set in a strikingly attractive campus among undulating hills. The fine work on the ceiling of the main library* right, *is particularly beautiful.*

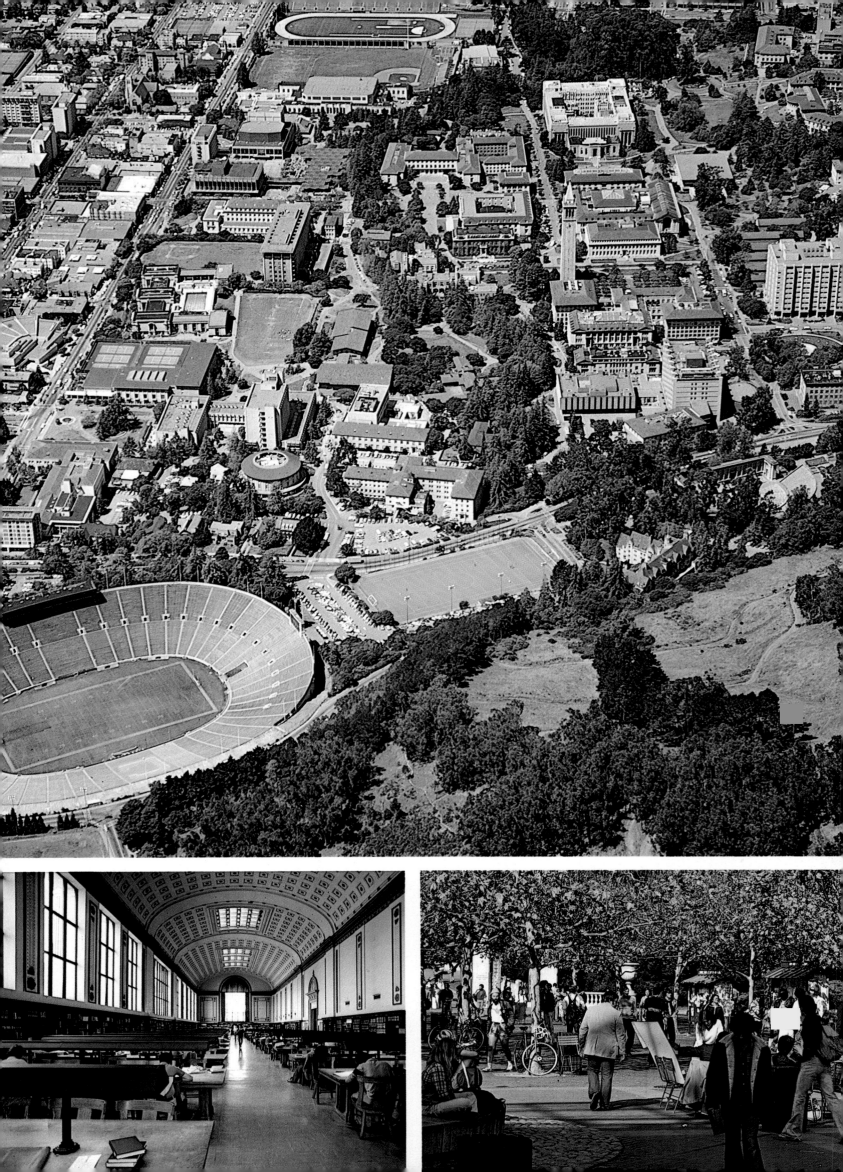

Sailing is a popular form of relaxation for city-dwellers and Marina District *left*, provides moorings within easy access of the city center. At the western end of the district the Palace of Fine Arts *above right*, rises like an ornate bubble.

The Renaissance architecture of the City Hall *above*, home to the city's board of supervisors, is frequently referred to as a classically extravagant contrast to the ultra-modern design of many of the San Francisco buildings, among them, the Embarcadero Center *right*, which has added high-rise office buildings, shops and restaurants to the Financial Center or the Hallidie Plaza *below*, where weary shoppers can pause for a while.

In the Embarcadero Plaza *below right*, Vaillancourt's controversial sculpture composed of 101 concrete blocks points the way to the clock tower of the old Ferry Building, a reminder of the days when ferry boats carried traffic across the bay. The Oakland Bay Bridge *overleaf*, is the more modern link between San Francisco and Oakland, the neighboring city across the water.

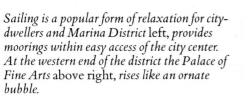

The Quality of Life

EVERY great city has its own lifestyle and character: Paris is the city of material and intellectual refinement, London of urbanity and sophistication, Venice is the result of the cultural collision of East and West. San Francisco, in a way, is Venice's modern equivalent.

Poised on the edge of the American Continent with nothing but the vast Pacific Ocean between it and the Orient and with powerful cultural ties with Europe, San Francisco is a place where ideas germinate and breed with enormous vitality. In terms of conventional culture it has led the way among American cities in the support of music and the theater, and on a more radical plane it has given rise to western American jazz styles, a particular form of abstract art, and has been a center of youth movements, such as that of the Beatniks and later the Flower Children.

In its more radical moods it seems to find inspiration in the philosophies of the East and its esoteric cults have based themselves on metaphysical concepts about man that are a challenge to the robust materialism which has always been the substance of the American way of life.

In between the extreme social conservatism of the first-nighters at the Opera and the radicalism of youth lies a vast range of human attitudes which can be traced back to the various influences that have been at work in the city's life since it was founded. It was only natural that those who became people of property after the Gold Rush should have felt it a duty to bring law and order to the city to protect private property and the individual. By doing so, they set themselves apart and became the 'society' of San Francisco. Many of them had been brought up in European traditions, so it was inevitable that they should want San Francisco to emulate the most civilized cities of Europe, and they set the pattern for what some may call cultural snobbery, but which is an essential link in the development of a lifestyle.

The Opera, the first to be municipally supported in America, the Symphony and the Ballet are cultural activities with which all who consider themselves part of the San Francisco elite want to be associated, but they also give enormous pleasure to those who have no mink to wear on opening nights or who arrive on bicycles instead of in Cadillacs. Moreover, the radical stream of San Francisco thought is always apparent in the modern and often experimental production and staging of many of the works.

The San Francisco Symphony Orchestra is internationally famous and is always under the direction of a conductor of international repute. As well as giving concerts, it appears with the Opera and the Ballet and in summer it attracts an audience of San Franciscans of all ages and walks of life to its open-air concerts at the Sigmund Stern Memorial Grove. These are the occasions when art loses the exclusiveness of which it is sometimes accused and becomes what the artist intends it to be, a form of expression for all the people.

The people's art is, of course, visible everywhere for few cities have such a large populaton of artists and craftsmen at work and displaying their products in the art galleries and art boutiques all over the city. Though much of it is aimed at the tourist who is looking for a cheap but original souvenir, there is much that is of a very high standard.

In the museums which, along with some of the best art galleries, are to be found in the Union, Geary and Sutter Streets area, San Francisco has noteworthy collections of Old Masters and of modern art. The former, which include Rembrandt and Rubens, are housed in the M.H. de Young Memorial Museum in Gold Gate Park and the latter at the Museum of Art in Van Ness Avenue. The twentieth-century giants are well-represented here, including Picasso, Matisse, and other members of the School of Paris, and there are fine examples of the abstract art of West Coast America which was pioneered here.

Above all, the quality of San Francisco's cultural life is embodied in the ideas that it has generated and, because ideas are the stock-in-trade of writers, these remain in the works of the poets and novelists who are either San Francisco born or have made the city their home.

The most romantic of these are Robert Louis Stevenson and Jack London; the most amusing Mark Twain. Several notable writers started their careers as newspapermen in San Francisco, among them Ambrose Bierce and Sinclair Lewis.

In more recent times, the city can claim William Saroyan and John Steinbeck, whose famous novel *Cannery Row*, was set farther down the coast at Monterey. From the radical side of the literary world have come Allan Ginsberg, and Jack Kerouac of the Beatnik era.

Though the literary and artistic fever has cooled since those days when Vietnam was the iron that seared the national mind, cultural undercurrents continue to swirl about the city streets, eddying into some bars where jazz and poetry readings hold an audience's attention or surging up in some offbeat theater or at some gathering place where over a bottle of wine or glass of beer San Franciscans continue to examine their own origins for the answers to the problems of the world.

A carefully restored house dating back to the Victorian era left, is the envy of many San Franciscans, who delight in this means of retaining contact with the city's past.

As night falls on San Francisco's Oakland Bay Bridge overleaf, the tranquil waters reflect the glow from the glittering lights along the shoreline.

Oakland Bay Bridge on these pages and overleaf is the world's largest steel bridge, jointed in midbay at Yerba Buena Island by a tunnel of enormous dimensions. At night what is really a superbly dovetailed pattern of bridges glimmers with a thousand lights against the most spectacular sunsets.

The distinctive outline of San Francisco below right, stands silhouetted against a brilliantly colored evening sky.

The Business City

THE rich and romantic history of San Francisco and its attractions for present-day tourists obscure the fact that the city's principal raison d'être is trade. Born as an outpost for shipping, bringing immigrants and imports to the new west of the United States and a departure point for cargoes of hides and tallow from the interior, San Francisco has grown with the industries that have developed in the Bay area.

After the Gold Rush and the discovery of silver in Nevada the city benefited from the cultivation of land in the rich valley between the Coastal Range and the Sierra Nevada. Here, the first ranches raised cattle and then the fruit farms produced the crops that grew abundantly in the Mediterranean-type climate. In the valleys around the Bay the European immigrants planted vines and made the landscape resemble their own homelands in France, Italy and Spain. The fruit gave rise to canneries and this provided more employment. With the increase in population there arose the need for the services provided by banks, insurance companies and entrepreneurs.

As an outpost, San Francisco continued to extend its port facilities, but when the railways arrived at Oakland, on the east side of the Bay, they created competition for the port. The goods that arrived by train were unloaded at this important city and sent across to San Francisco by steamer, but those earmarked for export were embarked directly on the ships sailing away across the Pacific.

When the Oakland Bay Bridge was built in 1936 and was followed by the Golden Gate Bridge, San Francisco gained a new means of communication with mainland America and the movement of goods by road took on an impetus which continues to the present day.

Efficient transport is essential to the present-day city with its active business life; many of its business workers live in other parts of the Bay and commute to work on the Bay Area Rapid Transport system which joins Oakland and San Francisco by a tunnel under the waters of the Bay. BART, as it is known, is one of the most modern transport systems of any U.S. city and links up not only Oakland, but Berkeley, Concord and other East Bay cities as well.

Other transport services providing for business people are the Municipal bus services, known as the Muni, and the famous cable cars which are more than merely a tourist attraction and are much in use along their routes which serve Powell, Bay, Hyde, Beach and California Streets.

The first of these famous cars ran in 1873 and was an invention of Andrew Hallidie, a wire rope manufacturer who conceived the idea of having an endless cable under the street to which the cars could be attached. This system is still very efficient in dragging cars up and down San Francisco's hills. Despite one attempt to withdraw the cars from service, it is likely that they will continue to serve both the businessmen of San Francisco and the tourists far into the future.

In the financial district, served by the California line cable car, the buildings are the tallest in San Francisco and make a mini-Manhattan which includes the headquarters of the Bank of America and the Pacific Coast Stock Exchange, a body that keeps its hours related to those of Wall Street despite the time zone difference between East and West coasts.

Most of the tall buildings are of recent origin, since the ever-present earthquake hazard caused a reluctance to build above twenty stories in the past. New, modern anti-seismic construction makes it possible to erect high-rise buildings, and among the tallest in San Francisco are the Bank of America's fifty-two stories and the unusual pyramid-shaped Trans-America Corporation building which has 48 stories.

It is here among the skyscrapers that San Francisco's financial world operates, dealing in the world's money markets and providing the usual financial services to the industries and small businesses of the Bay Area.

Of all the city businesses, the most abundant are the retail and service industries, an indication of the importance of the tourist industry which attracts millions of visitors each year from America itself and from overseas.

San Francisco's shops, particularly those in the area around Union Square, are stocked with products from all over the world and represent a big import business for the San Francisco docks. Most of the famous international names are present in this elegant part of the city: Charles Jourdan, the French footwear designer; Gucci from Italy, Jaeger of London. There are also many local manufacturers and designers whose flair in fashion and jewelry design helps swell the tourist revenue received by the city.

Many shops devote themselves to individual products of an esoteric nature. There is, for example, a place in Chinatown which concentrates exclusively on the sale of kites of every conceivable color and design; another specializes in almonds prepared in an ingenious variety of ways; another devotes itself to period dolls, and yet another to seashells. The city's retailers include those sidewalk vendors, reminiscent of the Beatniks and Flower Children, who lay out the belts, necklaces and other jewelry which they hope to sell to the passing tourist.

The core of the tourist industry centers on the catering and accommodation businesses, and San Francisco has developed these to high levels. At the top are world-famous hotels like the Hyatt Regency, a modern hotel of striking design overlooking the Embarcadero center and the Sheraton Palace, where Enrico Caruso was staying at the time of the great earthquake. The central court restaurant beneath its vast glass and iron dome is as splendid today as it was in 1906.

With the development of industry in other parts of the Bay area and the growth of Los Angeles as an industrial city, San Francisco has become more and more a center of finance and tourism; both are big business in a world where international money dealings and world travel are facts of life and San Francisco is well placed to thrive on both activities.

Six lanes of traffic roar across the famous Golden Gate Bridge left.

Unforgettable in the tranquility of the night, sunset floods the Oakland Bay Bridge overleaf.

Although a poor imitation of the original Barbary Coast which emerged in the days of the original Californian 'Gold Rush', with its blazing lights, bars, clubs and restaurants on these pages and overleaf, *still attracts innumerable visitors who flock to the city that introduced 'topless' entertainment to America.*

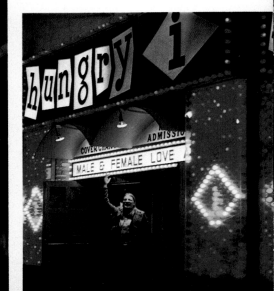

Many objections were raised to the initial building of the Golden Gate Bridge on these pages. "The Golden Gate is one of nature's perfect pictures…let us not disfigure it", wrote one of San Francisco's newspapers in 1930. Yet, quite apart from its more practical functions, the bridge has proved to have a poetry of its own. Shrouded in the low-hanging cloud of a San Francisco morning overleaf, it possesses the air of mystique which has made it a symbol of the city and the inspiration of authors such as Alistair Maclean.

Night in Bay City

WHEN work stops in San Francisco, fun begins and it takes a variety of forms, each one stamped with the idiosyncratic personality of the city itself. San Francisco can boast 2,500 restaurants of every nationality, striptease bars, singles bars, piano bars and jazz clubs, but few of the glittering international floor shows that are the trademark of the great tourist capitals of the world. And, strangely enough, there is no all-night revelry, for the city shuts down after 2 a.m. and peace reigns except for the occasional scream of a police car or, on foggy nights, a symphony of fog horns in the Bay.

Much of the nightlife of San Francisco – and there is plenty of it – exists to satisfy the large number of visitors who, like the miners of old, come into the city for some amusement and a drink or two in convivial company. Today, the pleasures are less vicious though they are perhaps no less rowdy. In fact, in the North Beach area, modern electronic devices push the decibels far above any noise level that the rowdiest pleasure seekers of the Barbary Coast could have created.

North Beach is the razzmatazz tourist area where street vendors, hawkers and neon lights all conspire to create an atmosphere of noise and confusion that excites the milling throngs who walk the streets in search of a good time. This is the typical tourist beat where just to walk about the streets is to participate and to feel that something is happening; a very different kind of night world from the downtown hotels and nightclubs where an elegant evening out begins with a drink at one of the bars with views over the glittering lights of the city and the velvety darkness of the Bay.

Top of the Mark at the Mark Hopkins Hotel on Nob Hill has been the universal image of this kind of eagle's nest cocktail lounge for years, but there are others, like the Starlite Roof and Henri's, with just as fantastic views for the price of a drink. At the Penthouse in the St Francis Hotel, which is right on Union Square, the center of downtown, patrons can enjoy the sights from the Golden Gate to Oakland Bay Bridge.

After the aperitif hour comes the dinner hour and this can go on until midnight when the food is good and the conversation sparkling. Most San Franciscans, like all people who appreciate good food, prefer to keep the eating and the entertainment separate, although the variety of restaurants and their menus might be considered entertainment in themselves. Dinner at a restaurant is usually followed by a visit to a night club or piano bar.

As in most great cities, French cuisine is highly regarded in San Francisco, and the most luxurious restaurants offer French menus along with elegant settings that suggest the splendor of the Belle Époque. Not unexpectedly, most of these restaurants have French names such as L'Étoile and L'Orangerie. The one exception is Ernie's whose plain, down-to-earth name is hardly in keeping with the splendor of the décor which not only reflects the golden era of San Francisco, but actually includes furniture and fittings from the great mansions of Nob Hill. There are also more modest establishments where one can enjoy cuisine bourgeoise and where the names are appropriately plainer though the food is not.

Since Italians are so numerous and their talents in the art of gastronomy are so renowned, their restaurants are legion, the menus endless with every kind of pasta, often homemade, and the atmosphere crackling with the noise and vitality that seems to be generated naturally in every Italian establishment.

Chinese restaurants abound, of course, both in and outside Chinatown, and there are Korean, Philippine, Japanese and Polynesian eating places as well as every kind of European variety.

On a warm summer night, most visitors wander down to the Fisherman's Wharf area where seafood is the speciality. At various places the diners sit outdoors and the scent of grilling fish and shellfish fills the air. If you don't want to sit down to a meal you can buy food at the sidewalk stands that sell takeout shrimp or boiled crabs that the attendants will crack open for you. Like most harbor areas, Fisherman's Wharf has a slightly seedy, rundown look but that is part of the atmosphere, too; that and the amazing variety of humanity which congregates there.

After a good meal, there is the late-night life to be savored – perhaps a disco or floor show type of entertainment, or that very San Francisco-style amusement, the piano bar. These bars vary in elegance and price but fundamentally they work on the principle that everyone likes a good drink and a bit of music or singing to go with it. As the night wears on the singing is often provided by the voices of the patrons who give voice to the golden oldies with enthusiasm and lack of tune.

Like any tourist town, San Francisco has its share of topless bars (where, it is claimed, bras were first discarded), hostess bars, massage parlors and prostitution. Much of the latter can be found in the area known as the Tenderloin, south of Union Square, and it is no different from such quarters anywhere in the world: a pale shadow of the Barbary Coast's roistering past, but as wicked as it dares to be in our liberal times.

But for most San Franciscans, now as then, the evening is simply a time to relax, to meet friends in their homes or in neighborhood bars, to become absorbed in a game of dominoes or mahjong, to stroll in the squares or along the waterfront or to do as the rest of the world does and watch television, and so to bed.

The Victorian Conservatory left, with its outstanding collection of flora is set in the Golden Gate Park, a beautiful stretch of parkland wrested from what was once a wasteland of rolling dunes.

Edith Coolbirth Park provides a panoramic view of San Francisco by night overleaf.

Cable cars on these pages and overleaf are the rolling symbols of San Francisco, for this is the only city in the world with an operating cable car system. Legend has it that Andrew Hallidie, a London-born engineer, was moved to invent the system by compassion for the beasts that supplied the power for the old horse cars.

In 1869, watching an overworked horse slip and fall as it hauled a heavy load up one of the city's steep slopes, he vowed to stop such cruelty and built the Clay Street Railroad Company. Since then the design has not changed…the cars still have no engines but are hoisted along by means of a steel cable permanently moving at a speed of 9½ miles an hour.

The precipitous slopes of San Francisco's hillside streets on these pages and overleaf afford magnificent views of the city and the bay beyond, and a stately ride in a cable car is an ideal alternative to an arduous climb on foot.

Cathedral
Grove

Chinatown, my Chinatown

OUTSIDE of Singapore, San Francisco has the largest Chinese quarter in the world. It covers 24 blocks and has all the characteristic architecture of the Orient, while suffering from the kind of traffic problems that are unmistakably Western in origin. The best way to get around Chinatown, therefore, is on foot.

In this way, one becomes a part of the environment, just one more among the swirling crowds that gaze into shop windows and gape at the amazing fantasy of pagodas, painted balconies, colored lanterns and, at night, the neon lights that wriggle feverishly around the Chinese pictograms.

Chinatown was not always the colorful playground that it appears today. When the Chinese first arrived with the other Forty-Niners, they were penned in a ghetto in the wildest part of the Barbary Coast and rapidly became purveyors of opium and child prostitution. When the railway from Sacramento was built east to meet the Union Pacific, the labor used was mostly Chinese, largely because it was the cheapest available. This 'competition' increased the prejudice against the Chinese, who were constantly subjected to the assaults of hoodlums who were rife in San Francisco in the 1870s.

To protect themselves against attack and exploitation, the Chinese formed themselves into organizations, the most powerful of which were the Tongs, a kind of Chinese Mafia. Though starting as a means of self-defense, the Tongs gradually developed into gangs which were constantly at war with other gangs for control of territory and businesses. The Tongs used hired assassins known as hatchet men, because they disposed of their victims with axes, and by the turn of the century gang warfare had grown to such an extent that it was not unusual to find bodies lying about the streets.

The earthquake of 1906 put an end to the ghettos and when Chinatown was rebuilt it became a more respectable, though still colorful quarter of the city.

This became the Chinatown of today, an area bounded by Kearney, Bush, Mason Streets and Broadway and bordering the financial district to the east and Nob Hill to the west. The main street of Chinatown is Grant Avenue which leads up from downtown San Francisco to a green-tiled archway topped by dragons that is the symbol of Chinatown.

Straight ahead lies Old St Mary's Church, which was built of bricks frabricated in China but which looks slightly out of place in the Chinese atmosphere because of its Gothic style. A block away down California is St Mary's Square with a statue of Sun Yat Sen, the founder of modern China. This was the center of old Chinatown and is still a popular place for the Chinese, who sit in the sun or bring their children to play in this quiet haven.

In Stockton Street is the headquarters of the Six Companies, one of the guilds formed to protect Chinese interests in the bad old days, and not far away is the temple of Kwan Yin, Goddess of Mercy, to whom it is customary to offer biscuits and other delicacies.

The story of the Chinese in California is related at the Chinese Historical Society where relics of the past are preserved. Here, the faded photographs tell the story of hopeful arrivals and the opium pipes indicate the habits that they brought with them, which no doubt helped to soften the pain of disenchantment in the place they called the Great City of the Golden Hill.

Today, the suffering of the early years is forgotten; the San Francisco Chinese enjoy the rights of all American citizens and have a standard of living that is envied by their fellow Chinese in Asia. They even have a trade center in Grant Avenue, though this is small as it represents the business not of a nation but of the Chinese community. The trade center is a vast and colorful bazaar dominated by a large dragon which looks down on the shops where Chinese foods and ceramics, cooking utensils, scrolls, lanterns, fans, and other knickknacks that appeal mostly to the tourists who visit Chinatown may be bought.

Though very hardworking, the Chinese also find time for amusement and enjoy, among other leisure activities, the Chinese films that come to them from Hong Kong and are either romantic traditional dramas or the latest Kung Fu thriller. The Chinese also celebrate their traditional festivals, the most important of which is the Chinese New Year.

The New Year is celebrated on the twentieth day of the Twelfth Moon, usually in January, and lasts several days. For the Chinese, this is a time for renewal and looking to the future and is a happy period in which family ties are strengthened. During this time, evil spirits are kept away by the traditional Chinese method of lighting firecrackers to scare them off and the streets are decorated with bunting and lanterns. There are parades and music, acrobats, jugglers and conjurors, but the main event is the dance which features a long dragon of paper and cloth carried by men whose dancing feet carry the fearsome creature through all the Chinatown streets to the accompaniment of shouts and cheers from the spectators.

Needless to say, the festivities are accompanied by much eating and drinking, and the restaurants in Grant Avenue offer every kind of Chinese food from Peking's delicious crispy duck to Cantonese paper-wrapped duck and all the varieties of prawn, fish, pork and egg dishes that only the Chinese can make with such delicacy and flavor.

It is on occasions such as this that the wealth and variety of the cultures that make up San Francisco become apparent and that the value of the Chinese contribution to the city's personality is most appreciated.

In a cool canyon at the foot of Mount Tamalpais in Muir Woods National Monument, redwoods left soar towards the sky like the pillars of some vast cathedral.

Between manicured hedges and blossoming hydrangeas, Lombard overleaf, the most picturesque of San Francisco's streets, winds tortuously downhill between Leavenworth and Hyde.

San Francisco's geographical position and the city's development as the largest seaport on the West Coast combined to make it the 'Gateway to the Orient'. The result was 'Chinatown' on these pages and overleaf, the largest community of Chinese people living together with their own language, culture and laws, outside the Orient.

The original Chinatown, built up around Grant Avenue, was destroyed in the devastating fire of 1906 but was subsequently rebuilt and today this neighborhood with its distinctive architecture and customs still provides a fascinating glimpse of the Orient transplanted, albeit with some concessions made to the American way of life.

In the Golden Gate Park overleaf, a bronze Buddha looks benevolently upon the people of San Francisco, whose strength lies in their traditional tolerance and the diversity of their culture.

First published in Great Britain 1979 by Colour Library International Ltd.
© Illustrations: Colour Library International Ltd., 163 East 64th St., New York, N.Y. 10021.
Colour separations by La Cromolito, Milan, Italy.
Display and text filmsetting by Focus Photoset, London, England.
Printed and bound by SAGDOS - Brugherio (MI), Italy.
ISBN 0-8317-7679-X Library of Congress Catalogue Card No. 79-2122
Published in the United States of America by Mayflower Books, Inc., New York City
Published in Canada by Wm. Collins and Sons, Toronto